Praying Through
Psalm 119

A One Month Journey to a
Deeper Love for God's Word.

Martin & Lynnette Bonner

Copyright © 2013 Martin & Lynnette Bonner

Scripture taken from the New King James Version. Copyright © 1982 by Thomas Nelson, Inc. Used by permission. All rights reserved.

Cover design & picture by Lynnette Bonner

All rights reserved.

ISBN-13: 978-1490983066

Dedication

To those who took the time to invest in our lives and instilled in us a love for God's word.

Contents

Introduction   Pg 7

Day 1	Pg 9	Day 12	Pg 53
Day 2	Pg 13	Day 13	Pg 57
Day 3	Pg 17	Day 14	Pg 61
Day 4	Pg 21	Day 15	Pg 65
Day 5	Pg 25	Day 16	Pg 69
Day 6	Pg 29	Day 17	Pg 73
Day 7	Pg 33	Day 18	Pg 77
Day 8	Pg 37	Day 19	Pg 81
Day 9	Pg 41	Day 20	Pg 85
Day 10	Pg 45	Day 21	Pg 89
Day 11	Pg 49	Day 22	Pg 93

Introduction

This book was a long time in the making. The idea first came about when Lynnette felt led to pray Psalm 119 over our children. Soon after that the Lord laid it on Marty's heart to walk through Psalm 119 in a Bible study group at church. The two scenarios eventually melded together to form this book.

Using the Word of God to direct our prayers can give greater depth and direction to our experience of prayer. Part of that depth comes from realizing generation after generation have experienced the same concerns and longings we have, and as we read their cries in the scriptures, it strengthens our faith in God's revelation as Truth. Praying through the scriptures also helps insure our prayers are aligned with the heart of God. James 5:16 says, "The prayer of a righteous person is powerful and effective." It is our desire that as believers pray through this little study it will be powerful and effective to increase their love for God's Word. For in His Word there is Life.

This is in no way meant to be an exhaustive study of this Psalm. Instead, it is meant to be a launching point. A way to initiate thinking and prayer that will hopefully spur you, the reader, to further prayerful study of God's precious Word.

With four kids of our own, we know how busy life can be. Yet it is so important that we take time daily to refresh ourselves in the messages of Truth from God's Word. With that in mind, we wanted to keep each day's study short and concise. But by all means, if you find yourself searching out a string of Truth, don't feel you have to press on to the next lesson the following day. Take your time. Meditate. Digest. And let God's Word infiltrate your heart and bring change.

God bless you as you continue on this journey to becoming more like Him.

Marty and Lynnette

Day 1

Psalm 119: 1-8

ALEPH

¹ Blessed are the undefiled in the way,
Who walk in the law of the LORD!
² Blessed are those who keep His testimonies,
Who seek Him with the whole heart!
³ They also do no iniquity;
They walk in His ways.
⁴ You have commanded us
To keep Your precepts diligently.
⁵ Oh, that my ways were directed
To keep Your statutes!
⁶ Then I would not be ashamed,
When I look into all Your commandments.
⁷ I will praise You with uprightness of heart,
When I learn Your righteous judgments.
⁸ I will keep Your statutes;
Oh, do not forsake me utterly!

Prayer

Lord help me to remain undefiled and to walk in the law of the Lord.

May I keep Your testimonies and seek You with my whole heart.

Help me to do nothing wrong and to walk in Your way. May I obey fully!

Help me to be steadfast in obeying Your decrees. And not be shamed when I study Your commands.

Help me to praise You with an upright heart and learn Your righteous laws.

Give me an obedient heart and do not forsake me!

Things to Consider

- The key word for this section is blessed or happy. The writer declares how blessed are those who are blameless in the way of the Lord. Similarly, in verse 2 they seek the Lord with a whole heart (that is undivided). In verse 3 they "do no iniquity (injustice / wrongdoing)."

- Notice the switch in verse 4. Here the writer recognizes that he is not these things. Though he wants to be so, he falls short of such flawlessness, whole-heartedness, and lack of wrong doing.

- The writer also looks forward to a time in the future where he will do better and so, in verse 8, pleads for God's mercy. "Do not forsake me, utterly!"

- Which person am I? Am I like the Pharisees of old, thinking that I am complete and in no need of help? Am I perhaps projecting that image? Or, am I in need of God's mercy?

- While you work hard to teach others the ways of the Lord, be careful that you do not portray yourself as something you are not. Rather pray that the Lord will give you the grace to help them recognize their own need for God's mercy and saving grace.

- God's promise to us is that He will not leave us nor forsake us (Hebrews 13:5-6). Also, Jesus promised His disciples that He would always be with them even to the end of the age (Matthew 28:20).

- Make sure that you understand your personal need for the grace that we can have in Jesus and rejoice that God has answered that fear that rises in all our hearts: "Will he leave me?"

- You are never more blessed than to rest within the grace of Jesus by faith in his righteousness.

Notes

Day 2

Psalm 119: 9-16

BETH

⁹ How can a young man cleanse his way?
By taking heed according to Your word.
¹⁰ With my whole heart I have sought You;
Oh, let me not wander from Your commandments!
¹¹ Your word I have hidden in my heart,
That I might not sin against You.
¹² Blessed are You, O LORD!
Teach me Your statutes.
¹³ With my lips I have declared
All the judgments of Your mouth.
¹⁴ I have rejoiced in the way of Your testimonies,
As much as in all riches.
¹⁵ I will meditate on Your precepts,
And contemplate Your ways.
¹⁶ I will delight myself in Your statutes;
I will not forget Your word.

Prayer

Lord, help me to keep my way clean by taking heed to Your Word.

May I seek You with my whole heart and never wander from Your commandments.

Help me to hide Your Word in my heart, that I might not sin against You.

Help me to see the importance of Your Word.

May I continually praise You and declare it daily. Help me to rejoice in Your testimonies as I would in great riches.

May I meditate on Your precepts, contemplate Your ways, delight in Your Statutes, and never forget Your Word.

Things to Consider

- The first Hebrew keyword in this section begins seven of its 8 verses and that is the preposition "in." The second keyword is the word blessed.

- The main question is stated up front and that is, "How can a young man keep his way pure?" Of course the question and its answer apply to us all. The answer is found "in" many different aspects of our life that can be recognized in the word "way."
    - A way or path is a series of decisions with forks and branches that take us different directions for good or for bad. To clean the way is to cut out those branches or decisions that would lead us to bad things in our lives, evil.

- We all need to listen to God's Word. The Hebrew word "beth" can be pictured as a shepherd caring for sheep. He feeds, waters, watches over, guards, and keeps the sheep. So we need to gather the Word of God and nurture, protect, and meditate upon it. But ultimately, we need to act according to it.

- We need to seek God, verse 10, rather than wandering after the things of this world. How difficult this truly is!

- Verse 11 points out that we need to hide the Word of God in our heart to protect against sin. To put the Word of God in our heart is more than just memorizing, although that is a good practice. It involves spending time hearing, reading, listening to, and meditating upon God's Word.

- Further points are given: verse 13 **rejoice** in God's ways like riches, verse 15 **meditate** and

contemplate God's Word/ways. Lastly, verse 16, to **delight** in God's Word and **not forget** it.

- The sooner we do all these things the better. How much grief and evil can be avoided by wisely listening to these words?

- Another thing to notice is that in verses 15 and 16 there is more of a declaration of what the writer will do. Recognizing the importance of God's Word in making our way pure, he makes the resolution to meditate, contemplate, delight in and not forget it.

Notes

Day 3

Psalm 119: 17-24

GIMEL

17 Deal bountifully with Your servant,
That I may live and keep Your word.
18 Open my eyes, that I may see
Wondrous things from Your law.
19 I am a stranger in the earth;
Do not hide Your commandments from me.
20 My soul breaks with longing
For Your judgments at all times.
21 You rebuke the proud—the cursed,
Who stray from Your commandments.
22 Remove from me reproach and contempt,
For I have kept Your testimonies.
23 Princes also sit and speak against me,
But Your servant meditates on Your statutes.
24 Your testimonies also are my delight
And my counselors.

Prayer

Lord, deal bountifully with me that I may live and keep Your Word.

Open my eyes to see the wondrous things in Your law.

May I remember that I am a stranger here as You open my eyes to Your commandments.

Oh that I would long for Your judgments at all times.

May I not stray from Your commandments and become proud, or cursed, so I will need no rebuke. And as I do that, remove reproach and contempt from me.

Teach me to meditate on Your statutes and may Your testimonies be my delight and counselor.

Things to Consider

- Key words in this section are to "deal bountifully" and "stranger," or more to the point, a "sojourner."

- This is reminiscent of the patriarchs who dwelt in Canaan as nomads – those who did not have a permanent place and yet God blessed them.

- The writer prays for God to pay him "good," as a servant is rewarded, so that he may live to keep God's Word.

- It is an interesting idea that God might hide his commandments from someone. There is an aspect to God that does not cast pearls before swine. For God to open our eyes to His Word is a grace. If Biblical concepts seem hard to grasp, we ought to pray for grace rather than despise what we do not understand.

- In verse 20 he speaks of his heart broken or shattered with longing for God's judgments. This world gives precious few righteous judgments. This grievous weight fills our hearts with longing for God's judgments to be brought forth. All the righteous hope Jesus will come down and settle his judgments upon all the earth. We look not for the judgments of men to fix things, but rather the judgments of God. This makes us strangers, sojourners, even in our earthly homeland.

- The writer highlights the oppression and persecution that often comes to those who stand for God's ways. The righteous seek God's Words as faithful counselors, but the world seeks out its own ways and casts reproach and contempt upon the righteous.

- We must navigate the tension of being called out of the world and yet given the task to reach people in the world. This takes a love for God and a love for others. This is not an easy tension to remain under. Our tendency is to move towards one or the other. Or to think that we are loving God when we have moved away from His true heart. God is not willing that any should perish but that all should come to repentance.

- Am I a stranger in this world or has it become too much my home? Am I like Lot's wife, so close to salvation and yet fixated on that which God is destroying, instead of looking forward to His destination for us? God help us to love Him rather than the world, but to also see the heart that He has for those who are trapped, imprisoned, and crushed by the enemy of all mankind.

Notes

Day 4

Psalm 119: 25-32

DALETH

^{25} My soul clings to the dust;
Revive me according to Your word.
^{26} I have declared my ways, and You answered me;
Teach me Your statutes.
^{27} Make me understand the way of Your precepts;
So shall I meditate on Your wonderful works.
^{28} My soul melts from heaviness;
Strengthen me according to Your word.
^{29} Remove from me the way of lying,
And grant me Your law graciously.
^{30} I have chosen the way of truth;
Your judgments I have laid before me.
^{31} I cling to Your testimonies;
O LORD, do not put me to shame!
^{32} I will run the course of Your commandments,
For You shall enlarge my heart.

Prayer

In hard times, Lord, may I be revived by Your Word. Teach me Your statutes.

Help me to understand the way of Your precepts as I meditate on Your wonderful works.

When my soul melts from heaviness, strengthen me according to Your Word.

Remove from me all lying, and graciously grant to me Your law as I choose the way of truth and cling to Your testimonies.

O Lord, do not put me to shame!

May I run the course of Your commandments as you enlarge my heart.

Things to Consider

- Some key words in this section are "Cling" and "Way."

- The writer starts out by noting that he tends to "cling" or stay with the dust and then asks for God to revive him. This contrast between clinging to dust and being revived by God is the spiritual principle of this world's way versus God's way.

- This lowliness of our nature looks to spiritual renewal and physical resurrection.

- We are going to see a contrast between "my ways" and the ways of God. The ways of God are revealed in His Word, law, precepts, and statutes.

- Notice the apparent contradiction in verses 29 and 30. How is it possible to need to be removed from the path of lying and yet say you have chosen the path of truth? Do we sometimes choose against the desires of our heart? How might this tie in with dying to our self?

- In verse 30 the writer says that he has laid out the judgments of God before him. In a sense he has spread them out so that they are easier to see and understand. Why might this be important and how can we do that?

- In verse 31 the word "cling" is used not of the dust but of God's Word. It does not seem to be a transition but rather a recognition that there is a part of him that clings to this earth. But there is another part of him that has chosen to cling to the Word of God that is God's witness of Himself and His ways. This highlights why he asks not to be put to shame. We can name those things that are our shame, but only God can deliver us from them.

- In verse 32, God's commands are a course, a track, on which we should run. But to do so we need God to touch our hearts. In fact they both reinforce each other. God uses his Word to "broaden" or deepen our heart so that we can embrace more of it and run its course better.

- Remember God did not lead Israel to the Promised Land by the way man would choose in the natural. He chose a different path. Choose God's way, choose life.

Notes

Day 5

Psalm 119: 33-44

HE

*33 Teach me, O LORD, the way of Your statutes,
And I shall keep it to the end.
34 Give me understanding, and I shall keep Your law;
Indeed, I shall observe it with my whole heart.
35 Make me walk in the path of Your commandments,
For I delight in it.
36 Incline my heart to Your testimonies,
And not to covetousness.
37 Turn away my eyes from looking at worthless things,
And revive me in Your way.
38 Establish Your word to Your servant,
Who is devoted to fearing You.
39 Turn away my reproach which I dread,
For Your judgments are good.
40 Behold, I long for Your precepts;
Revive me in Your righteousness.*

Prayer

Teach me, Oh Lord, the way of Your statutes, and help me to keep them to the end.

Give me understanding so that I will keep Your law and observe it with my whole heart.

Make me walk in the path of Your commandments and delight in Your Word.

Incline my heart to Your testimonies, not covetousness.

Turn my eyes from useless things and renew Your way in me. Establish Your Word in me and may I be devoted to fearing You.

May I dread Your reproach and never have to face it, and recognize that Your judgments are good.

Help me to long for Your precepts and revive righteousness in me.

Things to Consider

- More than any keyword, this section has a key concept and it is seen best by looking first at verse 40. The word "behold" points to the writer's need for God to look upon him. If God does not see our need and help us then we have no hope.

- A good picture to have in mind would be Hagar in Genesis 16. She had run away, distressed by Sarah and her situation. It was here that God spoke to her and she called Him, "The God Who Sees." Do I recognize my need, as desperate as Hagar's, for the God of heaven to see me and help me?

- Each verse looks to God to enable the writer in some way. In fact the verbs are formed in a way that asks God to cause it to happen. The writer sees his own inability in each of these needs.

- Verse 33 **Teach** me or cause me to be taught. How does God teach us? Do I always listen and learn? The writer pledges to "keep" God's statutes to the end. This picture is not just a statement of intended obedience. It's root literally means to guard and protect the teaching of the LORD concerning his way to its end. Where is this way of the LORD taking us?

- Verse 34 "Cause me to **understand**" leads to the next step. We need teaching but then we need to grasp it, to have that "Aha!" moment in which something becomes our own. Note the concept of a whole heart. Check out Jeremiah 3:10 and Jeremiah 29:13. What do you see?

- Verse 35 "Cause me to **walk**" recognizes the tendency to veer from God's path. What are the ways in which I tend to veer from God's path? Lord help us to walk with You.

- Verse 36 "Cause my heart to **incline/stretch out towards** Your testimonies," speaks of our desires and the things that draw us. What does the Bible have to say about our hearts? See Jeremiah 17:9.

    o What does my heart "stretch out towards" that it should not? Do I believe God can help turn my heart?

- Verse 37 "Cause my eyes to **turn/pass by**" points out the temptations in this life. Temptations are empty, worthless things. But they can draw our eyes. What are the things that cause my eyes to linger? Are they empty things I should pass over, that steal my spiritual life?

- Verse 38 "**Establish your Word**." Here the picture is one of God causing His promises to be strengthened or even kept. How we need God to Keep His Word to His people. What would happen to us if He did not keep it?

- Verse 39 "Cause my **reproach to be turned away.**" It is not stated whether or not he deserves these reproaches. Here he looks to God's mercy and goodness. In what ways do I need His mercy?

Notes

Day 6

Psalm 119: 41-48

WAW

*41 Let Your mercies come also to me, O LORD—
Your salvation according to Your word.
42 So shall I have an answer for him who reproaches me,
For I trust in Your word.
43 And take not the word of truth utterly out of my mouth,
For I have hoped in Your ordinances.
44 So shall I keep Your law continually,
Forever and ever.
45 And I will walk at liberty,
For I seek Your precepts.
46 I will speak of Your testimonies also before kings,
And will not be ashamed.
47 And I will delight myself in Your commandments,
Which I love.
48 My hands also I will lift up to Your commandments,
Which I love,
And I will meditate on Your statutes.*

Prayer

Let Your mercies come to me, Oh Lord – Your salvation according to Your Word.

Give me an answer for those who reproach me because of my trust in Your Word and don't take Your Word from my mouth. May I hope in Your ordinances.

Help me to continually keep Your law, forever and ever, as I walk in freedom and consider Your precepts.

May I speak of Your testimonies before those in authority and never be ashamed.

May Your commandments elicit delight and praise, and may I love them.

Help me to meditate on Your statutes.

Things to Consider

- This section begins with a focus on what the writer needs from God but then moves to a focus on what the writer will do in response. This sense of God and man in a relationship where both are "doing" gives a picture of the connection that God desires with us all.

- Notice how verse 41 ties salvation together with God's mercy. Godly people under the Old Covenant readily recognized their need for God's mercy (loving-kindness) in order to have salvation, both eternal and temporal.

- In verse 42 we are pointed to God's mercy as a thing that helps us to "answer" those who slander or reproach us. Have you answered this for yourself in your own heart? We must first be convinced of God's mercy before we can "answer" others.

- In verse 43 the "word of Truth" can also be thought of as the appropriate word, the word of understanding. The need for a word of truth is not just as opposed to a lie, but also as opposed to no word at all (nothing to say), or even worse, something foolish. Having a word of truth for the appropriate moment, is a grace of immense value. Do I hold my tongue until I know for sure God has given me understanding? "Ordinances" means the decisions or judgments of God.

- There is a natural flow in verses 41-44. The Word of the Lord needs to flow from our heart to our mouth and into our actions. It should affect how we relate to everything. What things tend to get in the way of this?

- But what can be meant by keeping God's Law forever and ever? As individuals we have the hope of resurrection which will allow us to do this. Remember, keeping is more than just doing, it involves guarding and nurturing.

- Notice these 5 things that the writer expects because his trust is in God.

    o The first is that he will **walk at liberty.** Freedom is both simple and complex. Those who freely sin find themselves bound by it and those who build up command upon command in order to never break God's law also become bound. So what is freedom? Free from the tyranny of our flesh and its desires. Free because I do not run from God's Word but to it. Free because I do not love this world (1 John 2:15-17).

    o He will **speak of Your testimonies**. The apostles prayed for boldness from God to speak the truth (Acts 4:29). Often our tongues are restrained from speaking because of fear. Boldness cannot be pretended. Thus the declaration that he will not be ashamed. Am I bold? What fears may hold me back? Can I give them to Jesus? If I ask then will He not supply His Spirit?

    o He will **delight..in Your commands.** Not only will he choose to delight in them, but they will literally be his delight. It is when we delight in the wrong things that the commands of God become an unpleasant thing to us.

- - Verse 48 can be seen as a **diligence in his duty**. He won't be lazy or slack in doing what God has called him to do.
  - Lastly, he will **meditate on God's statutes.** This implies a careful, thoughtful, consideration. He will remain humble and inspect his life against God's prescriptions.
- What a list! God too desires for us to be free, bold, delighted in Him, diligent, and humble.

Notes

Day 7

Psalm 119: 49-56

ZAYIN

⁴⁹ Remember the word to Your servant,
Upon which You have caused me to hope.
⁵⁰ This is my comfort in my affliction,
For Your word has given me life.
⁵¹ The proud have me in great derision,
Yet I do not turn aside from Your law.
⁵² I remembered Your judgments of old, O LORD,
And have comforted myself.
⁵³ Indignation has taken hold of me
Because of the wicked, who forsake Your law.
⁵⁴ Your statutes have been my songs
In the house of my pilgrimage.
⁵⁵ I remember Your name in the night, O LORD,
And I keep Your law.
⁵⁶ This has become mine,
Because I kept Your precepts.

Prayer

Lord, remember Your Word to me – the Word in which You have caused me to hope.

May it be my comfort in affliction, the giver of life.

When the proud hold me in great derision, may I never turn aside from Your law.

Help me to remember Your judgments of old, and comfort myself in them.

When the wicked forsake Your law, may I be indignant.

As I walk this pilgrimage may Your statues be my song.

My I remember Your name in the night and keep Your law.

And may Your Word become mine as I keep Your precepts.

Things to Consider

- The word "remember" is key in this section. Of course remembering implies an earlier knowing.

- The writer first recognizes that he needs God's help to remember. Both in what specifically needs to be remembered and in regard to our human weakness (am I even seeking to remember).

- In verse 50 he recognizes that times of affliction (humbling circumstances) can get in the way. It is in times of difficulty that we especially need to be reminded of God's Word. It is our hope. Is there something specific in my life today in which I need God's comfort? The Word of God makes us alive as the Holy Spirit brings it into memory.

- What makes affliction so oppressive is that those who are the main source of it are smug, proud and derisive in their cutting comments, whether to us or about us. The writer is tempted, but resists turning from the Law. How do I resist the temptation to disregard the Lord's command to me when I am derided by proud men? Why is pride so unappealing and able to provoke us?

- Verse 52. It is one thing to ask God to help us remember. But here the writer actively participates in this. It has been said that it is easier to steer a moving ship. It is good to ask God for help, but we also must do our part. Do I partner with the Holy Spirit in the things I pray for? What are some practical ways I could do this? Specifically, the judgments of God in the past comfort us in the present. God will put down the proud and lift up the humble.

- It is interesting in verse 53 that he is indignant that the wicked forsake God's law. In a sense this serves as a definition of the wicked – those who forsake God's law. Am I more angry that people have sinned against me or that they flaunt the laws of God? In contrast God's laws have been the "songs" of the writer. Songs are those things that speak to and of our heart. Does God's Word sing in my heart?

- The house of my pilgrimage is a term that points back to the patriarchs: Abraham, Isaac and Jacob. They were pilgrims and often were under the eye of the wicked. But God puts a song in our heart from his Word. Is my life on this earth like the "pilgrimage" of the patriarchs? Am I at home here or not?

- Lastly, the writer remembers the Lord's name. Does he specifically mean the covenant name YHWH? If so the fact that God is what He is, never changing, is a comfort. Of course all the different names of God speak of His nature and are comforting to us. In fact the writer speaks of this comforting remembrance as his possession. God intends me to not just read about being comforted by His Word and reminded of His nature. He desires me to have it as my very own experience. How can this happen?

- Have I come to be comforted by the very nature of God myself? What did I go through that helped me to see God's unchanging good nature was my true hope?

Notes

Day 8

Psalm 119: 57-64

HETH

*57 You are my portion, O LORD;
I have said that I would keep Your words.
58 I entreated Your favor with my whole heart;
Be merciful to me according to Your word.
59 I thought about my ways,
And turned my feet to Your testimonies.
60 I made haste, and did not delay
To keep Your commandments.
61 The cords of the wicked have bound me,
But I have not forgotten Your law.
62 At midnight I will rise to give thanks to You,
Because of Your righteous judgments.
63 I am a companion of all who fear You,
And of those who keep Your precepts.
64 The earth, O LORD, is full of Your mercy;
Teach me Your statutes.*

Prayer

Oh Lord, You are my portion! Help me keep Your words.

I beg Your favor with my whole heart, be merciful to me according to Your Word.

Help me to think about my ways, and keep my feet turned to Your testimonies.

May I hasten and not delay to keep Your commands.

When the cords of the wicked bind me, may I not forget Your law.

At midnight, may I rise up to give You thanks because Your judgments are righteous.

May my companions be those who fear You and keep Your precepts.

Your mercy fills the earth. Teach me Your statutes.

Things to Consider

- In this section the writer focuses on having the favor and the loving kindness (mercy) of the Lord.

- He first states that the Lord is his portion. This is reminiscent of the Levites. There is no indication that the writer is a Levite and has this in mind. But rather the writer seems to be saying that, of all the portions he could desire or seek in life, God is his focus. Am I satisfied with God himself being my portion if I had to lose everything to have him?

- There is a heavy focus on the writer's attempts and activities at drawing the favor of God to him.

    - First he **entreats God's favor**, simply praying for it and desiring it. Notice in his prayer he is cognizant of his need for mercy, which is God's nature.

    - Then, verse 59, he **thinks about his ways and changes them** based on God's Word. It is easy to say we love Jesus. But do we analyze our choices and decisions based on His Word and change? Now we can see why mercy is prayed for.

    - In verse 60 he is quick and **speedy to make those changes**. Procrastination is another way of saying I don't really want to do this. God help us to be careful to respond to His Holy Spirit diligently and boldly.

    - In verse 61 the writer first inserts what the wicked are doing. They are tying him up with their wicked deeds. However, he **hasn't forgotten God's law**. When we are sinned against our flesh wants to throw God's Truth out the window. It has a "binding" effect upon our ability to say yes to God's Spirit- and in a sense purposefully forget God's law.

- What things could be binding me and holding me back today? Are there things of the past, or things of the present that cause me to forget?

- In verse 62 he **gives thanks to God**. Whether it is in thanks for His judgments on my behalf or in general, we should all be thankful to God to the degree that we would have no problem rising at midnight to do it. Most likely he is still up at midnight because of the wicked mentioned earlier. In the midst of struggling in prayer is the heart of thankfulness. Does thankfulness sometimes get dropped from my prayers and heart?

- In verse 63 the writer points out that **he connects himself with those who fear God**, as opposed to the wicked. We may have dealings with the ungodly. But, those we are companions with and connect to in a spiritual way say a lot about our heart. Am I a companion or "associate" of people who fear God or those who love evil? All new believers have to come to grips with this question.

- Everywhere we look we can see the loving kindness of God surrounding us. Just in His provision of natural resources alone, we are swimming in it. How easy it is to lose sight of His mercy. God's prescriptions in His Word are intended to maximize our experiencing of His mercy. But we need to be taught.

Notes

Day 9

Psalm 119: 65-72

TETH

⁶⁵ You have dealt well with Your servant,
O LORD, according to Your word.
⁶⁶ Teach me good judgment and knowledge,
For I believe Your commandments.
⁶⁷ Before I was afflicted I went astray,
But now I keep Your word.
⁶⁸ You are good, and do good;
Teach me Your statutes.
⁶⁹ The proud have forged a lie against me,
But I will keep Your precepts with my whole heart.
⁷⁰ Their heart is as fat as grease,
But I delight in Your law.
⁷¹ It is good for me that I have been afflicted,
That I may learn Your statutes.
⁷² The law of Your mouth is better to me
Than thousands of coins of gold and silver.

Prayer

You deal with me just as Your Word says You will.

Teach me good judgment and knowledge. Help me to believe in Your commandments.

Help me not to stray and have to be afflicted. May I keep Your Word.

You are good and do good. Teach me to do the same.

When the proud lie about me, help me to keep Your precepts with my whole heart. I long to delight in Your law.

When I am punished help me to see the good in it, that I might learn Your statutes.

May I recognize that Your law is better for me than all the riches in the world!

Things to Consider

- Repeatedly throughout this section we are reminded of the goodness of God. However the section also brings up one of the paradoxes of life. Good can come from evil.

- Didn't God create all things good? Did He create anything evil according to Scripture? Somehow evil broke forth from the good that God had created.

- The good news is that this works conversely, as well. There is a mystery to how God enables good to come out of bad things. Read Romans 8:28-31. Now ask yourself, which is more important, whether bad things happen to me or that I am called according to God's purposes? How might I be letting the occurrence of bad things take on a greater importance than I should?

- The writer declares that God has dealt well with him. However, he goes on to mention affliction several times. In fact, it appears that proud men had created some lie about him and were circulating it publically. Paradoxically, the writer is saying, "God you let this bad thing happen, but it was good for me." How could it have been good for him?

- How do difficult things teach us not to stray from the Lord (verse 67)? Like the prophet Habakkuk, we too can be perplexed that God will use people more wicked than us to discipline us. How might we prepare ourselves for times of discipline that seem unfair?

- Verse 68 gives a declaration that God is good and does good things. However, does life ever cause me to question that? How might the declaration from God Himself that He is good help us to deal with the "bad stuff" of life? May the Lord help us to simply trust His heart for us even when we don't understand; to know He is good.

- The image of a heart that is "as fat as grease" is used. Clearly this is a metaphor. To have a heart that is either encased in fat or like grease is to have a heart that is insensitive to God and His Spirit. The heart requires circumcision (see Romans 2:29) so that it might respond to God's Truth. Heat and cold are critical to fat and its properties. When cold, fat congeals; hardens. When heated, it softens; melts away. How might spiritual heat and cold affect the spiritual "fat" condition of our hearts?

- In verse 71 the writer not only declares that affliction did him good, but that it taught him God's statutes (His prescriptions about life). We don't always understand why God prescribes a certain way of life. How might affliction have taught the prodigal son more about God's prescriptions in life?

- Is God's Word more valuable to me than great wealth? Do I spend more energy searching the Word of God for wisdom than working for earthly wealth? Is there something other than wealth that is more important to me than the Words of Life, which point to the Giver of Life Himself?

Notes

Day 10

Psalm 119: 73-80

YOD

*73 Your hands have made me and fashioned me;
Give me understanding, that I may learn Your
commandments.
74 Those who fear You will be glad when they see me,
Because I have hoped in Your word.
75 I know, O LORD, that Your judgments are right,
And that in faithfulness You have afflicted me.
76 Let, I pray, Your merciful kindness be for my comfort,
According to Your word to Your servant.
77 Let Your tender mercies come to me, that I may live;
For Your law is my delight.
78 Let the proud be ashamed,
For they treated me wrongfully with falsehood;
But I will meditate on Your precepts.
79 Let those who fear You turn to me,
Those who know Your testimonies.
80 Let my heart be blameless regarding Your statutes,
That I may not be ashamed.*

Prayer

Solidify my belief that You are the creator. Help me to understand and learn Your commandments.

May I hope in Your Word and find friends because of it.

When you punish me, may I understand that it's only because of Your faithfulness.

Let Your merciful kindness be the comfort promised.

May Your tender mercies give me life and may Your law be my delight.

Don't let me become proud or treat others deceitfully. Instead help me to meditate on Your precepts.

Don't let me break Your laws, so I won't be ashamed.

Things to Consider

- To be touched by the hand of God is a powerful thing. The Writer starts by recognizing God as creator. If God created us how should that affect our approach and our attitude towards Him?

    - At creation God "formed" Adam from the dust of the ground. This seems to imply a "hands on" fashioning.

- How are the Fear of the Lord and Hoping in God's Word related? Though we tend to think of fear as a negative thing, the proverbs say that the fear of the Lord is the beginning of wisdom. Have I "begun" to be wise?

- This section again recognizes that God afflicts us at times. But He does so in faithfulness. How could God "afflict" us and still be faithful? Have you ever had a child you corrected say, "You're being mean to me?" Do we respond that same way to God? Or do we trust God's heart for us?

- The hand of God can be upon us in ways we enjoy, and it can be upon us in ways we do not enjoy. But, either way He is always faithful. In times of affliction are we ever tempted to run from God? The same hands that bring discipline also hold hope, if we will humble ourselves before Him.

- The writer asks to be comforted by the Lord's "merciful kindness" and to live by His tender mercies. Do I dwell upon the mercy of God when I am in affliction? What are some of the merciful acts of God in Scripture that speak to me?

- The hands of man will often be harsh and unfaithful. They will often bring us grief with no comfort. But we can have the touch of God upon us even in these times. Let us humble ourselves under the mighty hand of God so that He will exalt us in the proper time (1 Peter 5:6).

- Last challenge, can God touch other people, who are going through difficult times, through us? Could I be the very hand of God in a person's life? The writer prays that those who fear God will look to him not because he is able to fix their problem, but because he can be a reminder to them of God's faithful love. How often do I consider that God wants me to be His love extended to those around me?

Notes

Day 11

Psalm 119: 81-88

KAPH

⁸¹ My soul faints for Your salvation,
But I hope in Your word.
⁸² My eyes fail from searching Your word,
Saying, "When will You comfort me?"
⁸³ For I have become like a wineskin in smoke,
Yet I do not forget Your statutes.
⁸⁴ How many are the days of Your servant?
When will You execute judgment on those who persecute me?
⁸⁵ The proud have dug pits for me,
Which is not according to Your law.
⁸⁶ All Your commandments are faithful;
They persecute me wrongfully;
Help me!
⁸⁷ They almost made an end of me on earth,
But I did not forsake Your precepts.
⁸⁸ Revive me according to Your lovingkindness,
So that I may keep the testimony of Your mouth.

Prayer

Oh Lord, give me a heart that would faint for Your salvation, one that hopes in Your Word.

May I search Your Word so diligently that my eyes grow weary when I need that special comfort only You give.

When I am shriveled and old don't let me forget Your laws.

When I am tired of living and others persecute me wrongly, may I remember the faithfulness of Your commandments. Be my help, oh Lord! Even when my end looms near, don't let me forsake Your precepts. Revive me according to Your lovingkindness and help me to keep the testimony of Your mouth.

Things to Consider

- This section reveals the ancient struggle for the righteous. They do not plot revenge on the wicked. Rather they cry to God for His salvation. This hope can be seen from an individual standpoint and from a universal standpoint. We need to be saved as individuals within our life time and we ultimately need to be saved as a whole, or mankind.

- Hebrews 11 states that not all the righteous receive physical aid in this life. Am I prepared for injustices in my life to continue, seemingly without God's notice? Is God failing in his faithfulness if this happens?

- The writer brings up the state of his soul. He is weary and fainting. His eyes are failing. Have you ever felt weary waiting on God's help? In 2 Corinthians 5:7 Paul says that we walk by faith and not by sight. Notice that the writer's eyes are failing but his faith is not. How does prayer help us when our eyes fail us? What difficulties did Paul face? (Hint: read 2 Corinthians 4.)

- In verse 83 a wineskin would be dried out and eventually shriveled up if left in smoke. Yet he battles to keep his faith.

- Verse 84 reflects the frustration that any of us would feel when faced with our own frailty. Waiting for God to help is not easy. Why is waiting for God good for us?

- Verses 85-87 reveal what the writer's problem is. Proud people are persecuting him. They devise plots to trap him and to "make an end" of him. Those who do such things do not take the time to see their actions from God's view. They plot and unleash evil on others, who, instead of doing so back, spend their time in tears before God seeking help. Would not a loving God eventually give justice, and sternly so?

- Verse 86. Though all men fail us, God is forever faithful. He can be trusted when all else fails. Why put our trust in anything else? What are the things that I tend to trust in besides God? Can they fail me (is it possible)? In fact, isn't it inevitable that they all will fail to be everything that I need them to be?

- Those who cry out to God shall be saved. (Acts 2:21) This is the promise we have from the Lord. The salvation may not be as we would picture it. But it is sure nonetheless. Why do I sometimes doubt this?

- When we keep our faith in God the wicked can't succeed in their desire to destroy us (God's people). Almost, but never completely. Thus the cry for life. The word revive literally means "cause me to live." Clearly this is not just about physical life.

- Ultimately, we need life from God. Man shall not live by bread alone but by every Word that proceeds from the mouth of God. Jesus is God's answer to this ancient cry. Has this been the cry of your heart? Have you found Jesus as God's answer to your cries both in the present and for your eternity? Jesus is your life.

Notes

Day 12

Psalm 119: 89-96

LAMED

89 Forever, O LORD,
Your word is settled in heaven.
90 Your faithfulness endures to all generations;
You established the earth, and it abides.
91 They continue this day according to Your ordinances,
For all are Your servants.
92 Unless Your law had been my delight,
I would then have perished in my affliction.
93 I will never forget Your precepts,
For by them You have given me life.
94 I am Yours, save me;
For I have sought Your precepts.
95 The wicked wait for me to destroy me,
But I will consider Your testimonies.
96 I have seen the consummation of all perfection,
But Your commandment is exceedingly broad.

Prayer

Remind me that Your Word is anchored in heaven, that Your faithfulness endures to all generations.

May I recognize Your faithfulness to all generations and know that You established the earth and keep it going.

Make Your law be my delight that I might not perish when affliction comes my way.

May I never forget Your precepts because by them You give me life.

Save me, oh Lord, for I am Yours. I seek Your precepts.

Even when the wicked want to destroy me, help me to consider Your testimonies.

May I see the perfection in Your exceedingly broad commandments.

Things to Consider

- The Hebrew Letter Lamed comes from the picture of an ox goad or cattle prod. It is the picture of authority and direction (teaching). God is our perfect authority and teacher, which is perfectly revealed in Jesus. Do I see Jesus and God's Word as the final authority on all of life?

- The writer begins by focusing on God and His works. All of creation was created by the "Word" of God. He spoke and it came into being. It continues to this day according to His ordinances. God as the author of all things is also the only qualified teacher for all things. Am I sometimes tempted to think that the thoughts of man are greater than the Word of God?

- We should also make the connection that the apostle John made in John chapter 1, when he reveals that Jesus is this Word of God. The Word of God is not just an idea or concept it is a Being who is one with the Father. He does not change. He has been set by the Father as the absolute Truth by which all things are to be judged. How does this world view the Word of God?

- In verse 91 the writer states that all things are God's servants. How could sin, wickedness, and even the devil himself be a servant of God? God did not create evil, but in the end, those who choose it cannot do anything other than further His purposes. Do I believe this? How might this change my trust in God's supervision of this world?

- In verse 92 it is mentioned that delight in God's law kept the writer from perishing. In what do I delight? How might those things put me in jeopardy both physically and spiritually?

- We obtain life by listening to God's commands as to a master teacher. Success comes through humble obedience. But success does not always mean an easy life as pointed out in verse 95.

- "I am Yours." We belong to God by right of Creation, but do we belong to Him by right of Devotion? Does my heart and soul belong to God not only because of a legal status but more because I love Him? Yes, God chooses us, however, our heart must respond and embrace that choice. Does my heart have other things that lay claim to its devotion?

- Verse 96 points to the things of this world. The perfection of any aspect of creation has its limits. But the commands of God are not limited. They reach to every generation in every nation with the same relevance and powerful veracity.

- How have advances in philosophy and technology caused mankind to think God's commands are no longer needed? Is it possible for the human race to advance or "progress" to a place beyond the need for God's Word? What dangers lie in the future with genetic manipulation and the post-human movement? Ultimately man will try to become God by his own hand. This will lead to destruction. Where does your trust find a foundation?

Notes

Day 13

Psalm 119: 97-104

MEM

97 Oh, how I love Your law!
It is my meditation all the day.
98 You, through Your commandments, make me wiser than my enemies;
For they are ever with me.
99 I have more understanding than all my teachers,
For Your testimonies are my meditation.
100 I understand more than the ancients,
Because I keep Your precepts.
101 I have restrained my feet from every evil way,
That I may keep Your word.
102 I have not departed from Your judgments,
For You Yourself have taught me.
103 How sweet are Your words to my taste,
Sweeter than honey to my mouth!
104 Through Your precepts I get understanding;
Therefore I hate every false way.

Prayer

Oh, give me a love for Your law! As I meditate on it daily, make me wiser than my enemies who are always with me.

Help me to meditate on Your testimonies and keep Your precepts.

Restrain my feet from every evil way, so I can keep Your Word.

Teach me, Oh Lord, so that I won't depart from Your judgments.

Let Your words be sweet in my mouth, sweeter than honey.

As I study Your Word and gain understanding, help me to hate every false way.

Things to Consider

- The focus of this section is clearly God's Word. Seven different words are used to refer to it and they follow a clear pattern: Law, Commandments, Testimonies, Precepts—Word, Judgments, Words (different in the Hebrew), Precepts (also different in Hebrew).

- Each of these refer to the Scriptures but from different facets of meaning. Briefly,
    - Law – the teaching or directions of God.
    - Commandments – the duties, charges, and orders of God.
    - Testimonies – God's witness about what is True.
    - Precepts – the statutes, appointments, even punishments of God.
    - Word (verse 101) – the speech, word, or sayings of God.
    - Judgments – pleading, avenging, condemnation, executions of God. (Picture a courtroom)
    - Words (verse 103) – speech, answers of God.

- The writer starts out by revealing that his love of God's law causes him to meditate on it all day. Meditation is to the Bible as digestion is to food. This is a process of prayerful reflection before God regarding His Law. Do I spend time even just once a day prayerfully reflecting before God about His Word?

- The blessings of meditating on God's Word are that the writer is wiser than his enemies. The Bible tells us to be as wise as serpents, but as harmless as doves (Matt. 10:16). Wisdom, however, does not mean you will lack enemies or persecution.

- Another blessing is that he is wiser than his teachers and even than the ancients before him. Many a young student has felt this way out of immaturity. But this is not the intent of the writer. He is elevating God's Word above the position of teacher and the reverence of age. Do you value God's Word above that of all earthly teachers both dead and alive? Jesus said He was greater than Solomon. Do we receive His Words as the very words of God?

- Ultimately, we need to let ourselves be taught by God. In the New Testament we are told that God gives us His Spirit to "guide us into all truth." God seeks to give you not just the Truth, but a love of the Truth. Do I look for the Lord's daily teachings to me? What is He teaching me today?

- Scripture is often referred to as sweet in the mouth. Several times in the prophets it later turns bitter, not because it is bad but because it speaks of judgment. When we are in right relationship with God, His Word is sweet. Is His Word sweeter than honey to me? Oh, Lord, forgive us for the many fleshly delicacies we run after.

- Twice (verses 101 and 104) he refers to a way that is not the Lord's way. First it is "every evil way." These are those ways that are not good and pleasant. The second is "every false way." These are the ways that appear good to our flesh, but in the end are evil. Are there ways that seem right to me, but in the end lead to something bad? How about ways that appear bad to me, but in the end are good? Whose definitions of "good" and "bad" are we using?

Notes

Day 14

Psalm 119: 105-112

NUN

¹⁰⁵ Your word is a lamp to my feet
And a light to my path.
¹⁰⁶ I have sworn and confirmed
That I will keep Your righteous judgments.
¹⁰⁷ I am afflicted very much;
Revive me, O LORD, according to Your word.
¹⁰⁸ Accept, I pray, the freewill offerings of my mouth, O LORD,
And teach me Your judgments.
¹⁰⁹ My life is continually in my hand,
Yet I do not forget Your law.
¹¹⁰ The wicked have laid a snare for me,
Yet I have not strayed from Your precepts.
¹¹¹ Your testimonies I have taken as a heritage forever,
For they are the rejoicing of my heart.
¹¹² I have inclined my heart to perform Your statutes
Forever, to the very end.

Prayer

Help me to recognize that Your Word is a lamp to my feet and a light to my path.

Oh Lord, I swear and confirm that I will keep Your righteous judgments.

When I am much afflicted, revive me according to Your Word.

Accept the praise I freely offer and teach me Your judgments.

My life could be snuffed out at any moment. Help me never to forget Your law.

When the wicked lay snares for me don't let me forget Your precepts.

May Your testimonies forever be the rejoicing of my heart, my heritage.

Incline my heart to perform Your statutes forever, to the very end.

Things to Consider

- The writer uses the picture of a lamp to illustrate the affect that God's Word has on his life. Today we would think of this as a flashlight. What are the dangers of not having a flashlight when it is dark? How might each danger be an example of parallel spiritual dangers?

- To have a flashlight is one thing, but to shine it in the direction you are headed and make a decision is another. Do I use God's flashlight in my life? When I do, do I correct my course according to God's Word or do I continue on, hoping to have my cake and eat it too?

- In verse 106 the writer does not see God's judgments or decisions as suggestions. He makes a vow before God that he will keep them. Do I hear God's Word on this kind of level? Is it another voice among many for me to hear but decide for myself? Is my commitment to the Lord strong enough that it no longer matters what I think, only that I keep my word to God?

- In the next verse we again see that the writer is "afflicted." Literally to be brought low or humbled. It is so bad that in verse 109 the writer's life is in his own hands. That is, his every move could put his life in jeopardy. In verse 110 the wicked have laid traps for him. Have you ever experienced something like this? How would you feel if others were trying to tear you down when you didn't deserve it?

- The response of the writer in this troubling time is to ask God to "revive" him. Literally to give him life. Have you ever been in a place where you felt dead? Did you cry out to God to put His life in you?

- The "free-will offerings" of our mouth is another way of picturing prayer. As they would bring a bull to be sacrificed before God to cover sins, so the writer offers up prayers to God that are voluntary. Have you ever noticed that there isn't a commandment to pray in the Law? Men ought always to pray, that is for sure. But it was not commanded. However, Paul later imperatively tells us to pray without ceasing for this is God's will.

    o Do I wait to pray until I am practically forced by the circumstances? How often do I freely offer up prayers to God? Do I only pray when I need something?

- In verse 111 the word heritage is used. It refers to that which is your portion or allotment. Do I view God's testimonies as my portion or the part that has been given to me? Are there particular things in this world that I am seeking to be my portion?

    o Am I satisfied with the portion I have been given? Why not? Would I truly be satisfied if I had a "greater" portion? How do I determine greater or better?

- Lastly, the wording here, of a heart that is inclined to do God's statutes, is actually stronger than we might think. It literally means to be stretched out towards. If my heart were a plant, in what direction is it growing or stretching? Towards God or this world? His Word or the philosophies and wisdom of this world?

Notes

Day 15

Psalm 119: 113-120

SAMEK

¹¹³ I hate the double-minded,
But I love Your law.
¹¹⁴ You are my hiding place and my shield;
I hope in Your word.
¹¹⁵ Depart from me, you evildoers,
For I will keep the commandments of my God!
¹¹⁶ Uphold me according to Your word, that I may live;
And do not let me be ashamed of my hope.
¹¹⁷ Hold me up, and I shall be safe,
And I shall observe Your statutes continually.
¹¹⁸ You reject all those who stray from Your statutes,
For their deceit is falsehood.
¹¹⁹ You put away all the wicked of the earth like dross;
Therefore I love Your testimonies.
¹²⁰ My flesh trembles for fear of You,
And I am afraid of Your judgments.

Prayer

Lord help me to hate the double-minded and to love Your law.

Be my hiding place and my shield. May I hope in Your Word.

As I keep Your commandments, keep evildoers from me.

Uphold me by Your Word, that I might live. And never let me be ashamed of the Hope I have in You.

When You hold me up I will be safe and I shall observe Your statutes continually.

Don't let me stray or be deceitfully false so You won't reject me.

Help me to love Your testimonies, because You put away all the wicked of the earth like dross.

Give me a holy fear of You and may I fear Your judgments.

Things to Consider

- It is easy to think of hatred as something that is always bad. But the Bible continually points us to hate that which is evil. The writer strongly rejects a divided heart or mind. What is double-mindedness and what is a divided heart? How can they cause trouble?

- Hating the double-minded is contrasted with a love for God's Word. People second-guess themselves but God's Word has been refined in the furnace seven times (Psalm 12:6). Are there parts of God's Word I don't love? Is it God who is wrong or me?

- Verse 114 gives us the beautiful picture of God as our shield and hiding place. He is all of that and more. However, God does not always shield our flesh. Why might God not protect us in the natural at times? Did God fail to shield Jesus? God is not just a lucky rabbit's foot for this life. He is a shield for our soul.

- The rest of this section focuses on God and His commitment to be a shield to those whose hearts are for Him and His Word. The writer hopes that God will uphold and support him because he is in danger of dying and being ashamed.

    - The life spoken of is more than just physical life. It involves the life of one's spirit that can only come from God. Have I ever felt ashamed for publically putting my hope in God? How we need his strength.

- The writer desires the "evildoers" to go away from him. He doesn't want to be in their company because of the coming actions of God. God will:

- - o   Reject them. They will have no place with him.
  - o   Put them away like dross in the refining of silver. They will be removed.
  - o   Judge. God is the judge of all. Thus the writer fears to be associated with evildoers.
- Jesus is the shield of God to all who do not want to perish with the evildoers of our generation. We are not called to physically separate ourselves from this world, otherwise no one could be saved. However, do I spiritually and emotionally separate myself from the thinking and actions of evildoers?
- The writer fears the judgment of God. Truthfully, we know that perfect love casts out all fear (1 John 4:18). However that is balanced by Philippians 2:12. "Work out your salvation with fear and trembling." Is there a proper place for fear in our understanding of the judgment of God?
- Do I allow God to refine me like silver by the work of His Word and Holy Spirit? Better yet do I yield and cooperate with this process?

Notes

Day 16

Psalm 119: 121-128

AYIN

^{121} I have done justice and righteousness;
Do not leave me to my oppressors.
^{122} Be surety for Your servant for good;
Do not let the proud oppress me.
^{123} My eyes fail from seeking Your salvation
And Your righteous word.
^{124} Deal with Your servant according to Your mercy,
And teach me Your statutes.
^{125} I am Your servant;
Give me understanding,
That I may know Your testimonies.
^{126} It is time for You to act, O LORD,
For they have regarded Your law as void.
^{127} Therefore I love Your commandments
More than gold, yes, than fine gold!
^{128} Therefore all Your precepts concerning all things
I consider to be right;
I hate every false way.

Prayer

Help me to do justice and live righteously, and do not leave me to my oppressors.

Be surety for me for good and don't let the proud oppress me.

May I seek Your salvation and righteous Word so long that my eyes grow weary.

Deal with me mercifully and teach me Your statutes.

Give me a servant's heart and understanding that I may know Your testimonies.

Oh Lord, so many regard Your law as void! Take action!

But help me to love Your commandments more than gold, yes fine gold.

Help me to consider all Your precepts concerning all things to be right and to hate every false way.

Things to Consider

- This section has the picture of a servant looking to his master and seeking the attention of the master. Although the servant only mentions his own eyes, it is clear that he is seeking the attention (eyes) of God.

- The first verse is his appeal. " I haven't oppressed others and yet they are oppressing me." His case appeals to his heavenly master to not "leave" him in the hands of his oppressors.

    - Are there times that we feel that God does not see our situation?

    - Scripture is clear that God does see us (Zech 4:10). Why might he delay in coming to our aid at times? How do I reconcile his delays with 1 Peter 3:12?

- Surety is the idea of backing up someone either financially or otherwise. What an idea that God could be the one who backs us up for the good. What are some of the failings that I need God to cover?

- In verse 123 the writer admits that his eyes grow tired from looking for God's salvation. The word for salvation here is Yeshuah, which is the Hebrew equivalent for Jesus. Have you ever grown weary looking for Jesus, and His help?

    - Jesus is God's Word of righteousness and salvation. Can I trust God to keep His Word?

- The servant recognizes that he needs God's mercy. This is sometimes translated as loving-kindness. However, notice he connects this with being taught God's statutes. When I don't understand why God operates as He does, do I ask Him to teach me? God in His mercy will teach us if we ask Him.

- In verse 125, the writer asks for understanding. In a sense he is asking for his own eyes to be opened to God's ways. Have you grown in your ability to understand God's ways?

    o Sometimes we can let our questions and doubts hang on us without dealing with them. Do I have any doubts today for which I need God's understanding?

- In verse 126 the writer makes it clear that the situation has gotten dire. Time is of the essence. How does God's timing differ from our sense of "good" timing? How might His all-powerful nature give Him a different view of when the "right" time to act is? Do I trust Him?

- The evildoers have made God's law to be broken and void. It is as if it doesn't matter anymore. Would this be an accurate picture of our country today? What would it look like if God were to act?

- The last two verses end in "therefore." This refers back to the timing issue. Although it is implied, the writer knows that God will act eventually. Therefore... Do I go after wealth (gold) and other "false ways" rather than waiting for God's intervention?

    o This picture is one of not giving up. Instead of losing faith, he continues to wait for God. And, instead of putting his hopes in the things of this world, he puts his hopes in God.

- When the Lord comes back will He find faith, in me? (Luke 18:8)

Notes

Day 17

Psalm 119: 129-136

PE

*¹²⁹ Your testimonies are wonderful;
Therefore my soul keeps them.
¹³⁰ The entrance of Your words gives light;
It gives understanding to the simple.
¹³¹ I opened my mouth and panted,
For I longed for Your commandments.
¹³² Look upon me and be merciful to me,
As Your custom is toward those who love Your name.
¹³³ Direct my steps by Your word,
And let no iniquity have dominion over me.
¹³⁴ Redeem me from the oppression of man,
That I may keep Your precepts.
¹³⁵ Make Your face shine upon Your servant,
And teach me Your statutes.
¹³⁶ Rivers of water run down from my eyes,
Because men do not keep Your law.*

Prayer

Lord, may I recognize how wonderful Your testimonies really are and may my soul keep them.

As I study Your Word, shine light and understanding where I need them.

May I long to keep Your commandments.

Have mercy on me, as You do to all who love Your name.

Direct my steps by Your Word, and don't let iniquity have dominion over me.

Redeem me from the oppression of man, and help me to keep Your precepts.

Look down on me and teach me Your statutes.

Oh that I would weep rivers when men don't keep Your law.

Things to Consider

- What are the things that fill me with wonder? Is God's Word one of those things? This "litmus" test is important for us to recognize. Notice in verse 129 that the writer mentions the soul. Is my keeping of God's Word more of an external thing or is it internal (heart and mind)?

- In verse 130 God's Word is an entrance or window to light/truth. In our natural self we are like a room with no windows - lacking light. When we hear or read God's Word it is an opening to Truth.

    - Jesus said He was the Light of the World (John 8:12). He who was the Word of God is the opening to Truth for all men.

    - The word "simple" is the idea of easily persuaded, or gullible. Have I allowed God's Word to open my mind and heart to Truth or have I been duped by the philosophies of this world? There is still hope if I turn to His Word.

- Life comes from God's mouth, but, in contrast, my mouth "pants" in longing for God's commands. Compare this to 1 Peter 2:2. What might cause my heart to not have a strong desire for God's Word?

- In verse 132 the writer desires God to recognize him and his need. Notice that it is God's custom (natural decision) to give mercy to those who love His name. What might it mean to love God's name? Has God made a "name" for Himself? Have others tarnished that name?

- In verse 133 the word "direct" is really more than that. It has a deeper meaning of establishing or making our steps firm. When your foot slips you stumble or fall. How is this a picture of sin and God's Word? Is there any sin that has dominion or power over me? A heart that desires to be free and prays for God's help is a key to freedom. Look at Genesis 4:7. It is clear that Cain failed to heed God's direction. What do you see in this passage about sin and our hearts?

- In verse 134 the writer doesn't just say "deliver me." Rather the word "redeem" is used. It is the idea that God would have to pay for me to be set free. In what ways does this tie in with Jesus? Will mankind be able to remove all "oppression" without Jesus? What things tend to support your answer?

- To have God's face "shine" upon you is to have His loving acceptance. The favor of God's acceptance, however, is tied to the favor of His teaching. Have you ever learned from a "master" in any profession? How was it helpful? How much more is Jesus the master?

- Just as my heart is tested by what it sees as wonderful, so I am tested by what causes me to weep. Does it grieve my soul when people dismiss God's ways? Does this grief necessitate anger and hatred towards them? To greatly weep over sin and yet greatly attempt to reach sinners with God's love is the way of God. How do I feel that I am doing in both of these counts?

    - Does God notice our tears? Can He empathize with them or is He unfeeling? Does God have emotions? Perhaps our sufferings in life only allow us to join God in His sufferings.

Notes

Day 18

Psalm 119: 137-144

TSADDE

137 Righteous are You, O LORD,
And upright are Your judgments.
138 Your testimonies, which You have commanded,
Are righteous and very faithful.
139 My zeal has consumed me,
Because my enemies have forgotten Your words.
140 Your word is very pure;
Therefore Your servant loves it.
141 I am small and despised,
Yet I do not forget Your precepts.
142 Your righteousness is an everlasting righteousness,
And Your law is truth.
143 Trouble and anguish have overtaken me,
Yet Your commandments are my delights.
144 The righteousness of Your testimonies is everlasting;
Give me understanding, and I shall live.

Prayer

You are righteous, O Lord. Upright are Your judgments.

May I recognize that Your testimonies are righteous and very faithful.

May zeal consume me when my enemies forget Your words.

Help me to see the purity of Your Word, and love it.

Even when I am small and despised, don't let me forget Your precepts.

Help me believe in Your everlasting righteousness, and know Your law is truth.

When trouble and anguish overtake me, may Your commandments be my delight.

Give me understanding of the everlasting nature of Your righteous testimonies, and I will live.

Things to Consider

- Righteousness is key throughout this section. Though the writer never refers to themselves as righteous, this is the picture of a righteous person. However, in light of God's righteousness our righteousness is not worth mentioning.

- God himself is the very definition of righteousness. All He does is right and just. The writer uses the word "upright" of God's judgments. What comes to mind when you think about a crooked judge? God's judgments, however, are straight , not twisted, or perverted. One can look on and see the clarity of them.

- If God is righteous then it stands to reason that His testimonies (Word) are righteous as well. However, notice the word "faithful" in verse 138. This means that it can be leaned upon or trusted and it will hold up. Though God's Word is faithful, people are not always so faithful. What might 2 Peter 3:16 say to us and our responsibility to God's Word?

- In verse 139 the word "zeal" is related to jealous. It is not a negative thing, but has the sense of a righteous anger at something being used improperly.

  - We see this zeal in Jesus in the cleansing of the Temple in Jerusalem. In today's terms we may fear coming across as too extreme. How might that fear affect our hearts?

  - If you have enemies it would be instructive to see how they live. If they do not listen to God's Word then it is not a problem that they fight against you, it is natural.

Romans chapter 1 states that mankind's problem is not that it doesn't have enough truth or evidence. Rather its problem is that it suppresses the truth.

- o Am I zealous for God's Word in my life or do I suppress its wisdom, direction, and instruction?

- God's Word is not just 99.99% pure. Psalm 12:6 says that it is like silver refined seven times. The use of seven is meant to imply completely refined, that is, no impurities. When I plan my own course I am redoing something that God has already done for me. His way is revealed for us to follow. Do I believe this?

- Verse 141. When we are small in our own eyes then we will look up to God and His Word. Am I okay with being small and looked down upon by the world? Or, must I make myself great in the eyes of the world? When King Saul became great in his own eyes he left God behind.

  - o How might John the Baptists words in John 3:30 address this situation?

- God is not righteous for a period of time. He is forever righteous. This is critical because we humans are not forever righteous.

- In verse 143 the writer mentions the trouble and anguish they have. Adversity and difficulty are part and parcel in this life. Isaiah 53 declares that Jesus was a man of sorrows and acquainted with grief. Does the grief of this world and the enemy of my soul kill my delight in God and His Word?

  - o It is righteous for a man to struggle against this present darkness in maintaining faith.

Am I still fighting this "good fight?" How might prayer be critical to this fight?

- The last verse repeats verse 142, but adds that we need insight and understanding to "live." Clearly the writer isn't just talking about staying alive physically, is he? Are there things that I do not understand? Instead of forsaking God's Words do I pray for insight?

Notes

Day 19

Psalm 119: 145-152

QOPH

145 I cry out with my whole heart; Hear me, O LORD!
I will keep Your statutes.
146 I cry out to You;
Save me, and I will keep Your testimonies.
147 I rise before the dawning of the morning,
And cry for help;
I hope in Your word.
148 My eyes are awake through the night watches,
That I may meditate on Your word.
149 Hear my voice according to Your lovingkindness;
O LORD, revive me according to Your justice.
150 They draw near who follow after wickedness;
They are far from Your law.
151 You are near, O LORD,
And all Your commandments are truth.
152 Concerning Your testimonies, I have
known of old that You have founded them forever.

Prayer

Lord, I cry out with my whole heart! Hear me! Help me to keep Your statutes.

When I cry out to You, save me, and help me to keep Your testimonies.

May I rise before the dawn and cry for help. May my hope be in Your Word.

May sleep never be more important to me than meditating on Your Word.

In Your lovingkindness, here my voice and revive me according to Your justice.

Those who follow after wickedness and are far from Your law are all around me.

Yet, You are near, O Lord. And all Your commandments are Truth. Ground me in the knowledge that Your testimonies have been founded by You forever.

Things to Consider

- This section focuses on the cry of the individual to God. The first verse mentions that the writer cries out with a whole-heart. What would a half-hearted cry be like? The writer's main desire is not that God would hear, but rather give an answer. Is there a real difference between believing God hears you and not believing He has answered you?

- In verse 146 the writer specifically cries out to God, "Save me." This is reminiscent of the cry, "Hosanna, save us," in the New Testament. "Save" here is asking for assistance, deliverance, and aid in the problem.

- Verse 147 points out that he is up before the dawn crying out to God, which really is a picture of prayer in times of stress. Have you ever encountered a time so stressful that you couldn't sleep? Did you turn to God in prayer during that time?

- Verse 148 in a similar way reveals that he stays awake throughout the night searching and meditating on God's Word. Perhaps the writer looks for an answer or looks for hope. Do I see God's Word as the only source of both answers and hope?

- The writer calls upon God's "loving-kindness" in verse 149. In a sense, he gently reminds God of His nature, hoping for help. To have a judgment or decision from the Judge of judges is to have life. In fact, in Jesus, God has decided that all who believe in Him will have everlasting life. Have I truly put my faith in the person and work of

Jesus? Is He my answer and hope for the trials of life and my own failings (sin)?

- Verses 150 and 151 contrast on the idea of nearness.

    o The first verse sees the approach or nearness of those who follow after "wickedness." They come close, which brings turmoil and trouble to the writer.

    o However, in the second verse the Lord is near in the sense of a personal relationship. How is my relationship with the Lord? Surely His Word declares that He is near to us (Hebrews 13:5), but am I near to Him? What might draw me away from my Lord?

    o The mention of Truth is in contrast to the Lies of the wicked. Which am I impacted by the most: The nearness of God and His Truth or the nearness of the wicked and their lies?

- In verse 152 the word "testimonies" is the idea of God's witness. God's Word is forever a witness of who He is, what He is doing, and what Truth is. God has forever gone on record in regard to the Truth. He is not a man to recant His testimony. What does this say to me about my own desire to embrace His witness?

Notes

Day 20

Psalm 119: 153-160

RESH

₁₅₃ Consider my affliction and deliver me,
For I do not forget Your law.
₁₅₄ Plead my cause and redeem me;
Revive me according to Your word.
₁₅₅ Salvation is far from the wicked,
For they do not seek Your statutes.
₁₅₆ Great are Your tender mercies, O LORD;
Revive me according to Your judgments.
₁₅₇ Many are my persecutors and my enemies,
Yet I do not turn from Your testimonies.
₁₅₈ I see the treacherous, and am disgusted,
Because they do not keep Your word.
₁₅₉ Consider how I love Your precepts;
Revive me, O LORD, according to Your lovingkindness.
₁₆₀ The entirety of Your word is truth,
And every one of Your righteous
judgments endures forever.

Prayer

Help me never to forget Your law and because of it deliver me from all affliction.

Plead my cause. Redeem me. Revive me by Your Word.

May I understand that salvation is far from the wicked, because they do not seek Your statutes.

Yet, great are Your tender mercies O Lord, so revive me according to Your judgments.

When many persecute me, help me not to turn from Your testimonies.

May those who do not keep Your Word disgust me.

Help me to love Your precepts. Take that into consideration and revive me according to Your lovingkindness.

Oh that I would get it through my head that the entirety of Your Word is truth and every one of Your righteous judgments will endure forever.

Things to Consider

- The phrase "revive me" occurs repeatedly throughout this section. God is the ultimate source of life. Moses told Israel that men shall not live by bread alone but by every word that comes from the mouth of God (Deuteronomy 8:3). He began all life and to Him we should look for it. Do I seek life in things other than God?

- The first part of this section refers to an affliction. "Consider it and rescue me," is the writer's cry. This is a picture of appealing to a judge.

- The next verse is a picture of appealing to an attorney. The writer literally asks God to argue his argument, plead his pleading, and take up his cause. When God is your defense you need not fear. Who can defeat Him?

    - Here again is the sense of being redeemed. It is more than just a vindication. There is a payment that needs to be paid. Have I recognized my own faults in my problem and called out to God? Am I presenting myself to Him as innocent or in need of redemption?

- In verse 155 the word "salvation" is the word "Yeshuah," which is the Hebrew equivalent of Jesus. The heart of God will not be close to the wicked in the sense of being on their side.

    - Notice that a sign of wickedness is a lack of seeking after or investigating God's statutes or prescriptions. How hard do I seek after God's prescriptions in order to know them and understand them?

- Verse 156 recognizes the great amount and great quality of God's tender mercies. However the writer desires that they be towards him. Some decisions of God may not appear to be tender and merciful to us. Can God be tender in mercy towards the humble and yet tough in judgment to those who are proud? Is this a contradiction? Why or why not?

- In contrast to God's great mercy, the writer has a great number of persecutors and enemies. Why might this cause someone to turn from God's testimonies?

- In verse 158 the writer sees and considers the treacherous individuals around him. This version uses the word "disgusted." It can have a range of meaning from hatred to grief. It is a heavy thing to be around those who could care less about what God thinks. They often act in contradiction to it. How do I generally deal with this?

- Verse 159 complements the first verse of this section. On the one hand the writer wants God to consider his affliction and on the positive side he wants God to consider his love for God's precepts. Each of these is his "case," which backs his call for being revived or literally being enlivened by God.

- We often approach truth through a path of deductive and inductive reasoning. The path hopefully ends at the truth. God's Word is not that way. From the very first Word, it is Truth. It is not trying to arrive at truth, but revealing it to us from beginning to end.

    o How does it make you feel knowing that the judgments of God revealed in His Word cannot be overturned?

- Some of those judgments we may like and some may cause us to fear. Are there any decisions that God has made in His Word that give you anxiety? If God's Word is Truth and will not be changed then how do I deal with that?
- Do I look to Jesus to give me new life by His Holy Spirit?

Notes

Day 21

Psalm 119: 161-168

SHIN

¹⁶¹ Princes persecute me without a cause,
But my heart stands in awe of Your word.
¹⁶² I rejoice at Your word
As one who finds great treasure.
¹⁶³ I hate and abhor lying,
But I love Your law.
¹⁶⁴ Seven times a day I praise You,
Because of Your righteous judgments.
¹⁶⁵ Great peace have those who love Your law,
And nothing causes them to stumble.
¹⁶⁶ LORD, I hope for Your salvation,
And I do Your commandments.
¹⁶⁷ My soul keeps Your testimonies,
And I love them exceedingly.
¹⁶⁸ I keep Your precepts and Your testimonies,
For all my ways are before You.

Prayer

Lord when those in authority persecute me without cause, may my heart still stand in awe of Your Word.

Help me to rejoice in it as one who finds great treasure.

Help me to hate and abhor lying, but love Your law.

All day long may I praise You because of Your righteous judgments.

May I recognize that those who love Your law have great peace, and nothing causes them to stumble.

O Lord, may Your salvation come. Help me to do Your commandments.

May my soul keep Your testimonies and may I love them exceedingly.

Help me to keep Your precepts and testimonies because all my ways are before You anyhow.

Things to Consider

- At the heart of this section is the struggle of the righteous under the persecution of the unrighteous. The writer points to "princes" who persecute him. Persecution from authorities can be extremely heavy. Has anyone ever used their position or authority to attack you in some way?

    o The first verse says that the princes do this without cause, but it can also mean that they are doing it for no reason or gain. How might that make it worse?

- "But" is a powerful word. In verse 161 the writer could respond in kind, but..... Do I have such an awe or reverential fear of God's Word that it keeps me from paying back wrong for wrong (1 Thess. 5:15)?

- In verse 162 the writer rejoices as if having found a great treasure. Look at Matthew 13:44-46. Do I see the gospel of Jesus as if it were a priceless treasure? What things in this life might cloud my insight in this matter?

- Verse 163 makes a strong statement of hatred towards lying and love towards God's law. Why are we so afraid to say that we "hate" sin in today's generation? Is it right to hate that which destroys everyone and everything? Do I see sin as exactly that?

- For some praising God even one time a week proves to be too much. What does praising God seven times a day say about the writer's heart and focus each day? We can praise God because His judgments are not crooked. To the contrary, they are just and right.

- The "great peace" of verse 165 is a precursor to the New Testament's phrase, the peace of God that surpasses all understanding (Philippians 4:7). Clearly this does not always mean peace between us and others. Do I have such an inner peace? Romans 5 says that in Christ we have peace with God. Am I at peace with God?

    o Those who have God's peace in their heart will not be made to stumble. This is a huge statement. Think about the story of Jacob's son, Joseph. Though he wasn't perfect, yet he didn't fall. Am I at peace with trusting God though things may not go the way I plan?

- Verse 166 uses the term Yeshuah for salvation again. Jesus is the salvation of the Lord and the one in whom we should put our trust. It is hope in Jesus that helps us to do His commands. What did Jesus say about His commands that He gave us (John 14:21)?

- In verse 167 the writer speaks of greatly loving the testimonies of God. Is the witness that God has given us in His Word something that I love exceedingly (i.e. to a great degree)? What things in my life may be competing for my affections?

- In the last verse we recognize that our ways are always seen by God. There is no hiding place from God. Do I consciously take note of this throughout the day, or do I live my day without regard to my heavenly Father? Why might I want to hide from God? Does hiding from God help us?

Notes

Day 22

Psalm 119: 169-176

TAU

169 Let my cry come before You, O LORD;
Give me understanding according to Your word.
170 Let my supplication come before You;
Deliver me according to Your word.
171 My lips shall utter praise,
For You teach me Your statutes.
172 My tongue shall speak of Your word,
For all Your commandments are righteousness.
173 Let Your hand become my help,
For I have chosen Your precepts.
174 I long for Your salvation, O LORD,
And Your law is my delight.
175 Let my soul live, and it shall praise You;
And let Your judgments help me.
176 I have gone astray like a lost sheep;
Seek Your servant,
For I do not forget Your commandments.

Prayer

Lord, let my cry come to You. Give me understanding of Your Word.

Let my supplication come before You and deliver me according to Your Word.

May my lips utter praise as You teach me Your statutes.

May my tongue speak of Your Word for all Your commandments are righteous.

As I choose Your precepts, be my help.

May I long for Your salvation and may Your law be my delight.

Give me life, and help me to praise You and recognize the help Your judgments give me.

When I go astray like a lost sheep, seek me out, for I never want to forget Your commandments.

Things to Consider

- Here we have the cry of a lost sheep seeking the help of the good shepherd (see John 10). When lost or confused, we often come to a crossroads of sorts. At this point we either cry out to God for help or plunge on down a troubled path. Do I see my own life as just such a story?

    - Even when we are believers and are eternally saved and "found," do we sometimes feel lost in regard to knowing what to do? What does it mean to see God as a "good shepherd" in these moments?

- Notice in verse 169 that his cry is more about understanding his situation than getting out of it. How does God generally give understanding? What about the timing of the understanding He gives?

- In verse 170 the writer now moves to asking that his supplication, or petition to be delivered, would be received by God. Notice that he ties deliverance to God's Word. How might God's Word be the key to our deliverance? Does he mean the Bible or some special prophecy we may receive from God?

- In verse 171 and 172 the writer turns back to his mouth and lips. James tells us that this aspect of our anatomy can get us into a lot of trouble (James 3). But its true purpose is to be a source of blessing. To praise God and actively speak about His Word blesses God.

- In verse 172 the writer looks to the "hand of God" for help precisely because he has chosen to follow God. Though this is metaphorical here, the prophets pick this metaphor up and use it for the Messiah as the Arm of the Lord, and the Right Hand of God. How might we think about our troubles differently if we truly thought God Himself would help us? Hasn't he?

- Verse 174, "I long for your salvation" (Again, the word used is Yeshuah.) Jacob, on his death bed, says just such a thing (Genesis 49:18). In the same way that the Old Testament believers waited for and longed for Messiah, so we too should have a heart looking forward. Do I truly long for the return of Jesus and God's salvation on this earth? What are my deepest heart yearnings?

- In verse 175 the writer throws himself on the mercy of the court. In light of verse 176 and his own going astray, he looks to God's mercy. Let me live and I will praise you! What promises has God made, in regard to Life, for those who put their trust in Jesus (John 11:25-26; 20:31)?

    o What do you think praise will be like in heaven? We do get a glimpse of it in the book of Revelation.

- Jesus was the good shepherd of God gone out to seek and save that which had gone astray. No one can believe on Jesus without first understanding this. When people sin against us, it is easy to lose sight of our own sin.

    o What situations or people have I kept focused on so that I wouldn't have to see my own sin? Does confessing my own sin let them "off the hook?"

    o May my heart desire to be sought out by God because that is exactly what He has done for me and intends to continue. What fears come to mind when I think about God seeking me out? What joys come to mind?

Notes

About The Authors

Martin and Lynnette Bonner live in the pacific northwest where Marty pastors an Assemblies of God church. They have four children. Marty, the son of a logger and a homemaker, grew up in the evergreen hills of Idaho. Lynnette, the daughter of missionaries, was born and raised in Africa. They met in college, and have been ministering together ever since.

You can learn more about their church and read and listen to Marty's sermons and Bible studies by visiting www.totallyforgiven.com/blog.

Lynnette also pens wholesome Christian Fiction....

Look For:

THE SHEPHERD'S HEART

BOOK ONE

*He's different from any man she's ever known.
However, she's sworn never to risk her heart again.*

Idaho Territory,

Brooke Baker, sold as a mail-order bride, looks to her future with dread but firm resolve. If she survived Uncle Jackson, she can survive anyone.

When Sky Jordan hears that his nefarious cousin has sent for a mail-order bride, he knows he has to prevent the marriage. No woman deserves to be left to that fate. Still, he's as surprised as anyone to find himself standing next to her before the minister.

Brooke's new husband turns out to be kinder than any man has ever been. But then the unthinkable happens and she holds the key that might save innocent lives but destroy Sky all in one fell swoop. It's a choice too unbearable to contemplate...but a choice that must be made.

*A thirsty soul. Alluring hope. An Oasis of love.
Step into a day when outlaws ran free, the land was wild, and guns blazed at the drop of a hat.*

And...

Islands of Intrigue: Book 1

She's been living a lie that could just get her killed...

Widowed former Hollywood actress Devynne Lang has been living a quiet life in the San Juan Islands of the Pacific Northwest. For years, she's hoped her fabricated death would keep her identity safe from the public, and more to the point, from the stalker who forced her into hiding. But strange things have been happening around her place and this time, with a daughter to protect, she can't afford one mistake – even if it means letting Carcen Lang get close enough to help.

Carcen would do anything to protect his brother's widow and her daughter. So when he discovers Devynne may be in danger, he vows to find the man responsible. But dead lead after dead lead frustrates and baffles. Until the unthinkable happens and he realizes the danger has been closer than either of them could have imagined.

...because lies always have a way of coming back to bite you.

Made in the USA
San Bernardino, CA
16 July 2013